LIGHTS, CAMERA, ACTION!

MAKING MOVIES AND TV FROM THE INSIDE OUT

LISA O'BRIEN

ILLUSTRATED BY STEPHEN MACEACHERN

Owl

Owl Books are published by Greey de Pencier Books Inc.,
179 John Street, Suite 500, Toronto, Ontario M5T 3G5

The Owl colophon is a trademark of Owl Children's Trust Inc.
Greey de Pencier Books Inc. is a licensed user of trademarks of Owl Children's Trust Inc.

Distributed in the United States by Firefly Books (U.S.) Inc.,
230 Fifth Avenue, Suite 1607, New York, NY 10001.

We acknowledge the generous support of the Canada Council for the Arts
and the Ontario Arts Council for our publishing program.

Author's Acknowledgements
The author would like to thank the Ontario Arts Council for its support;
Anne Tait for her wisdom and friendship; Sheba Meland for her encouragement;
Kat Mototsune for her keen editorial eye; Annabel Slaight for opening the Owl doors;
and Susie Feinstein, Mary Swinton, Shirley Stefaniuk and all the other agents
who introduced me to some really terrific kids.

Cataloguing in Publication Data

O'Brien, Lisa, 1963
Lights, camera, action! : making movies and TV from the
inside out

Includes index.
ISBN 1-895688-75-2 (bound) ISBN 1-895688-76-0 (pbk.)

1. Motion pictures – Production and direction – Juvenile
literature. 2. Motion pictures industry – Juvenile
literature. 3. Motion pictures – Vocational guidance –
Juvenile literature. I. MacEachern, Stephen. II. Title.

PN1995.9.P7027 1998   j791.43   C97-931758-4

Design & Art Direction: Julia Naimska

Printed in Hong Kong

A   B   C   D   E   F

CONTENTS

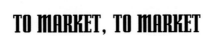

So You Want to Be a Star

You're at the movies watching your favorite actor on the big screen, or you're all set for your favorite television show to start. You wonder — could you be an actor in the movies or on television? Before you make the big leap towards stardom, there are some things you should know . . .

Come out to play

Acting is a craft, like playing music. Would you ever play guitar in front of an audience without proper preparation? It's the same thing with acting. You have to know the craft and properly prepare the role before you perform. Playing music or playing a part, there are some steps you have to take to play well.

Know the instrument

To play the guitar, the first step is getting to know your instrument. As an actor, you are the player. And your instrument is . . . you!

Know your sheet music

In music, the sheet music tells the musician the notes to play. In acting for movies, the screenplay tells the actors the words to say.

Play the music

If you picked up a guitar and just played the notes, without making the music loud and soft, without varying the tempo, without putting any emotion into it, the music wouldn't be very interesting to listen to. If an actor just read the lines, it would be pretty boring for the audience, too. If you are acting a character within a story, you have to bring all of yourself and your imagination into the lines you say to play the part well.

Popcorn Quiz

When did the first kid appear on screen?

(answers to Popcorn Quizzes on page 63)

ACTION!

MAKIN' FACES! • Sit in front of a mirror and imagine a series of emotional experiences. Study the expressions you make.

THE EYES HAVE IT • They say that eyes are the windows to the soul. Try covering up the rest of your face and see if you can communicate an emotion with just your eyes.

BODY TALK • We can express a lot by the way we stand or walk. Watch the way the people around you use their hands to express a thought or stand to show an attitude. Compare it with how you use body talk to express things.

SPEAK YOUR MIND • It's not so much what you say as how you say it. Next time you exaggerate while telling a story, notice how the tone and the rhythm of your speech are different from when you are telling the straight truth.

What's happening?

A good way to prepare yourself for acting is to become aware of what you're experiencing moment by moment. How do you feel when your teacher corrects you in front of the whole class? Compare that to what it's like to get an A+ on a math exam. What goes through your mind when you're in the dentist's chair? Or when you see a huge spider? Or when you're on a rollercoaster headed straight up . . .?!

Now, as an actor, how would you express it? It's not enough for an actor to just feel an emotion. Actors must actively express the emotions they're feeling.

DIRECTOR'S NOTE

WHO ARE YOU? BEFORE YOU STEP INTO THE SHOES OF A CHARACTER, IT'S BEST IF YOU START BY EXPLORING ALL THE SIDES OF YOUR OWN CHARACTER FIRST. TRY KEEPING A DAILY JOURNAL WHERE YOU CAN RECORD YOUR THOUGHTS AND FEELINGS. IN ACTING AND IN LIFE, ALWAYS TRY TO TRUTHFULLY EXPRESS THE QUALITIES THAT MAKE YOU UNIQUE.

SCREEN SPEAK

actor
Actors are chosen to bring to life the characters in a story presented as a performance.

character
A character is a participant in a story, either written or performed.

feature
A full-length film, generally about 120 minutes long.

role
The role is the character played by an actor.

short
A film that runs no more than 30 minutes. The very first movies were usually short films of one or two minutes.

THE BIG IDEA

From idea to screenplay: starting to create a make-believe world.

The Screenplay

Long before an actor is chosen to play a character — even before there's a story — the whole thing starts with an idea. Ever wondered how a screenplay gets written? Most of the time, it goes something like this:

From idea to script

1 Someone takes an idea for a movie to a producer, or the producer has an idea.

2 The producer hires a screenwriter to turn the idea into a script.

3 The writer spends a lot of time thinking about and researching the idea.

4 After many, many drafts, the screenplay is finally finished.

What is a screenplay?

Is a screenplay a blueprint? A story? A puzzle? It's all three!

A blueprint is a plan that gives the workers building a house a detailed picture of what they will be building. A screenplay is like a blueprint — it gives the director, the designers, makeup artists, camera people, props people, special effects people and actors a picture of the make-believe world they will create by making the movie.

A screenplay is a story told for the screen, with a beginning, a middle and an end. It is broken down into scenes, and these scenes are put together into acts. A scene can be any length, from a line or two to several pages, and it serves two purposes: it moves the story forward and it reveals character.

For the actors, the screenplay is like a puzzle. They search through it for clues that will help them understand the characters they will play. Each actor must find the answer to this question: Who is my character?

Popcorn Quiz

What is the fastest a feature-length film script was written for a major studio?

DIRECTOR'S NOTE

LOOK FOR THE ARC MOST STORIES ARE ABOUT CHARACTERS WHO GO THROUGH A SERIES OF EVENTS AND COME OUT CHANGED SOMEHOW. FOR EXAMPLE, IN THE MOVIE HOME ALONE, THE MAIN CHARACTER IS A KID NAMED KEVIN, A TIMID BOY WHO IS FED UP WITH HIS FAMILY. HIS FAMILY ACCIDENTALLY LEAVES HIM HOME ALONE, AND CROOKS TRY TO ROB THEIR HOUSE. KEVIN STOPS THE CROOKS AND LEARNS THAT HE'S BRAVER THAN HE THOUGHT, AND THAT HE REALLY LOVES HIS FAMILY. THE "CHARACTER ARC" SHOWS HOW THE CHARACTER CHANGES FROM THE BEGINNING OF A STORY, THROUGH THE MIDDLE, TO THE END.

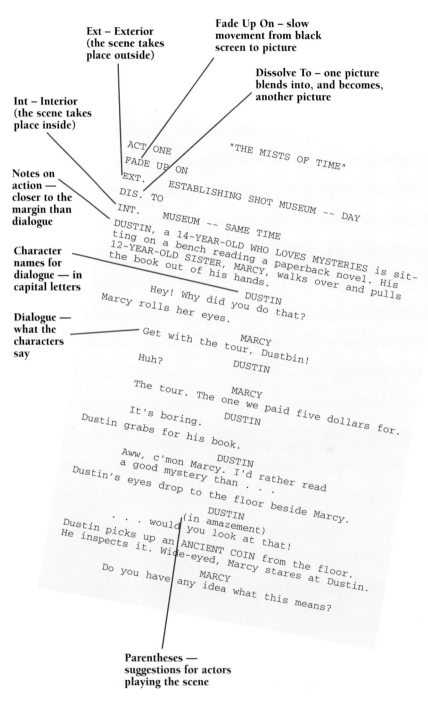

Ext – Exterior (the scene takes place outside)

Fade Up On – slow movement from black screen to picture

Dissolve To – one picture blends into, and becomes, another picture

Int – Interior (the scene takes place inside)

Notes on action — closer to the margin than dialogue

Character names for dialogue — in capital letters

Dialogue — what the characters say

Parentheses — suggestions for actors playing the scene

```
ACT ONE
FADE UP ON
EXT.                "THE MISTS OF TIME"
DIS. TO    ESTABLISHING SHOT MUSEUM -- DAY
INT.    MUSEUM -- SAME TIME
   DUSTIN, a 14-YEAR-OLD WHO LOVES MYSTERIES is sit-
   ting on a bench reading a paperback novel. His
   12-YEAR-OLD SISTER, MARCY, walks over and pulls
   the book out of his hands.
                    DUSTIN
        Hey! Why did you do that?
   Marcy rolls her eyes.
                    MARCY
        Get with the tour, Dustbin!
                    DUSTIN
        Huh?
                    MARCY
        The tour. The one we paid five dollars for.
                    DUSTIN
        It's boring.
   Dustin grabs for his book.
                    DUSTIN
        Aww, c'mon Marcy. I'd rather read
        a good mystery than . . .
   Dustin's eyes drop to the floor beside Marcy.
                    DUSTIN
                 (in amazement)
        . . . would you look at that!
   Dustin picks up an ANCIENT COIN from the floor.
   He inspects it. Wide-eyed, Marcy stares at Dustin.
                    MARCY
        Do you have any idea what this means?
```

9

Cast Away!

The screenplay is finished and the producer has raised the money to make the movie. The producer hires a director to bring his or her vision of the story to the screen. Now begins one of the most challenging parts of making a movie — finding the actors to play all the different characters. This is known as *casting*.

Direct casting

The producer and director hire a casting director, who chooses actors to fill all the roles in a movie or television series. That means finding the best actors for the least amount of money in the shortest period of time. Instead of gathering all the possible actors to play the parts, or going through them one by one in their minds, casting directors hold *auditions*. Auditions are like tests for actors. In an audition, the casting director, producer and director see how actors would look and act if they were chosen to play particular roles.

TALKING TO ANNE TAIT

casting director for movies and television shows

Q: What do casting directors look for when they audition an actor?
A: We look for the actor to be real and to be interesting. I personally like actors who show zip and humor. Actors could talk gibberish if they want, as long as the emotion is there. The words aren't as important in an audition. We're looking for character.
Q: Any advice for actors just starting out?
A: Keep practicing! Whether it's in a school play, or just reading out loud at home — anything that helps you to learn how to express yourself truthfully. Don't let anyone ever convince you to be fake!

Breakdown!

First, the casting director reads the entire screenplay very carefully. Extensive notes about all the characters and details of the script make up a *breakdown*. Look to the right side of the page to see what a casting breakdown for the screenplay of *The Mists of Time* might look like.

Popcorn Quiz

How many pages of screenplay does it usually take to make a movie?

From the Casting Office
CASTING BREAKDOWN

Movie: The Mists of Time

A family feature film telling the story of a brother and sister who are "super sleuths." After finding an old coin in a museum, they are transported back in time to ancient Egypt to solve a mystery from the past.

Shoot dates: Late July/early August. Agents send pictures and resumés right away!

We are currently seeking actors to play the two leads:

Dustin (age 14): A positive, energetic boy who loves adventure. Think of him as a young Sherlock Holmes: always on the move, searching for clues and constantly asking questions. Loves reading mystery novels and has, at times, an overly active imagination. When he and his sister find an ancient coin, it's just the fuel Dustin needs to start tracking down the origin of this mysterious artifact.

Marcy (age 12): Dustin's younger sister. She's a sensible girl who likes to look before she leaps. Marcy's a straight-A student who takes pride in keeping everything neat and orderly. She has inherited her mother's love for history and archaeology, but also has a sentimental, romantic side that occasionally appears. Although Marcy loves and looks up to her brother, she can be a typical "pest" at times to him.

DIRECTOR'S NOTE

LISTEN COMMUNICATION GOES BOTH WAYS. MAYBE YOU CAN ALREADY CLEARLY ARTICULATE YOUR THOUGHTS AND FEELINGS. BUT ARE YOU A GOOD LISTENER? WHEN PEOPLE TELL YOU STORIES ABOUT THINGS THAT HAPPEN TO THEM, CONCENTRATE ON WHAT THEY'RE SAYING. THEY'LL BE IMPRESSED IF YOU REMEMBER DETAILS.

Not-So-Secret Agent

How does the casting director find actors to audition for roles? By sending out the casting breakdown to the people who represent the actors looking for work — the agents.

Introducing Johnny

Every day, agents get breakdowns faxed to them by casting directors. Agents study each breakdown and try to match up the actors on their *rosters*, or lists of clients, to the roles that need to be filled.

If you want to get work acting in movies or TV, you probably need an agent. You want an agent to submit you for roles that suit you. The agent wants clients that stand a good chance of getting the roles they are sent to audition for. It's time for you to meet Johnny — he's a kid, maybe a lot like you, who wants to try his hand at acting. He went on one audition and didn't get the part, so now he's looking for an agent to help him.

Need an agent, get an agent

First Johnny checks the idea out with his parents. If they think it's OK, they can help Johnny find the names and phone numbers of some reputable talent agents who represent young actors in the area.

Johnny and his parents call the agents to see if they're taking on new actors. To the ones that are, they send Johnny's school picture or a snapshot, and an information sheet: Johnny includes his name, birthdate, height, weight, hair and eye color, any acting experience or training he has, and some of his skills and hobbies. He completes the package with a cover letter including his home phone number.

Johnny waits a week or two, then calls each agency to make sure they received his package. A couple of agents are interested enough to set up an interview.

Johnny keeps in mind that he has to feel as comfortable with the agent as the agent has to feel with him. His parents help him with this. They all have questions for the agents: How long have you been in the business? How many kids do you represent? What kinds of roles have your clients been cast in?

Finally, Johnny finds a good match both ways. Susie at the KidStar Agency "signs him up."

Say "cheese"

What Johnny needs now is a series of 8" x 10" black-and-white pictures, taken by a professional photographer. Susie suggests a good photographer to Johnny, and helps him put together a resumé. The resumé is typed on white paper and then photocopied. Photos and copies of the resumé make up packages that will get sent to casting directors in response to their breakdowns. Johnny is on his way!

Popcorn Quiz

How many actors auditioned for the role of Dennis in the Hollywood movie *Dennis the Menace?*

The lucky break

Johnny's agent calls him to say he has an audition. Before he gets off the phone, Johnny makes sure to write down and repeat back to his agent the name of the production, and the time and place of the audition. He asks her to send the script pages with the scenes he has to prepare. Now the real work is starting . . .

SCREEN SPEAK

agent

An agent works with actors, suggesting them for roles. Agents have to match up their clients to the roles that need to be filled.

casting

This is the matching up of actors with the characters or roles they will play.

casting director

Casting directors are hired to find actors to play the roles.

dialogue

This is the speech written for the characters in a scene.

director

The director guides the action of a film or TV show, is involved in almost every decision and maintains the creative vision of the project from pre-production through post-production.

producer

The producer is the one who brings together all the elements of a TV or movie project: money, schedules, crew, etc.

scene

A piece of action that takes place in a single location over a single period of time.

script/screenplay

Both are stories to be acted: the story for a live theater play is often called a script; a screenplay is for performance in a movie.

writer

The writer creates the story, the setting and the dialogue.

GETTING IT TOGETHER

During pre-production, the producer chooses the cast and crew, the craftspeople who will make the idea a reality. To find the actors, the casting director holds auditions.

Be Prepared

It might surprise you to learn that auditions are usually scheduled ten minutes apart. Ten minutes isn't very long to prove that you're the best actor for the role. So how do you do it? By the time you walk into that audition, you've prepared, and prepared, and prepared some more! Let's see how Johnny does it.

Taking sides

The script pages Johnny receives to prepare for the audition are called *sides*. He knows he's going to spend a lot of time with them over the next few days! They were faxed to him, so he photocopies them onto regular paper. He highlights all the lines of the character he's auditioning for.

Then Johnny starts working on straight memorization of his lines. He repeats them over and over again. Some people like to record them into a tape recorder, and then play them back. Johnny prefers to handwrite all the lines to help him memorize them. He makes sure he's completely familiar with the lines he will have to say in the audition.

Get real

It's the actor's job to be real in a make-believe situation. The screenplay supplies that situation to an actor in a movie. But you might only get a scene or two to work with. So to prepare for an audition, you have to guess at a lot of the information to get a clearer idea of the whole picture.

Look at the scene and ask yourself what led to that moment. What happened years before, months before, days before and, most importantly, the moment before this scene. Answering the question about the *moment before* gives you a springboard to start your audition in a fresh,

believable way. But remember, anything you imagine has to make sense with what is already there.

Hey, listen

The first key to acting is listening to what is said to you in a scene. The script tells you what the other character is going to say and how you are going to respond. But you have to make the words seem fresh, like you've just heard

them for the first time. Acting in a scene is reacting to what the other person is saying. Look below: a reaction can be many things — a reply in words, or an expression on your face, or even an action.

Whatever the reaction is, it has to be real. And the trick to reacting realistically is to really listen to what the other person is saying. That way you will be reacting to what's there, not what you expect to be there.

DIRECTOR'S NOTE

LUCK Luck, timing and talent are three important things in an actor's life. If luck and timing are on your side, you'd better be prepared so you can show off your talent.

ACTION!

Here's a listening exercise to help you hear and understand the lines in a scene. You'll need a friend or family member to help out.

> **DUSTIN**
> Hey! Why did you do that?
> **MARCY**
> Get with the tour, Dustbin.

READ • Read your line. "Hey! Why did you do that?"

LISTEN • Have your partner ask your line back as a question. "Why did I do that?"

REACT • You repeat your line to respond to the question. "Yeah, why did you do that?"

LISTEN • Listen to your partner read the other character's line. "Get with the tour, Dustin."

REACT • Repeat your partner's line back to them as a question. "Get with the tour?"

LISTEN • Listen as your partner repeats the line back to you. "That's right, get with the tour."

PAY ATTENTION • This exercise will help you listen for what is really being said.

Popcorn Quiz

What was the world's first full-length feature film?

17

Creating the Character

The actor has to breathe life into the character he or she is playing. To bring a character to life, the actor must try to understand what's behind the lines. So, take your sides and grab some paper and a pen. It's time to ask some questions about this character . . .

I am (character's name) Dustin Wright

Physical: I am (age, sex, height, appearance) a 14-year-old boy, tall for my age; I have curly red hair and freckles.

Sociological: I am (things like grade in school, details of home life, hobbies) an average North-American kid; in 9th grade getting average marks; living with my mother and younger sister; we have just moved to the city from living in small towns; an avid reader of mystery novels.

Psychological: I have (things like ambitions, attitudes) a lot of energy and an overactive imagination; I am creative.

I am unique because I would make a great sleuth, if I had a mystery to solve.

My relationship to the person I'm reading with is brother/sister.

It is (year, month, day, time) a Friday afternoon in September, late 1990s.

We are (where?) on a tour at the museum where my mom works.

I want this person to leave me alone so I can sneak away from the tour.

To achieve this goal, I am willing to sit here reading my book and acting antisocial.

Who and where?

Establish who and where you are from clues in the scenes you are given. Write a short autobiography for your character. Since we always adjust our behavior depending on who we are with, figure out the relationship between the characters in the scene. Now, imagine the surroundings. This will help you fill in the reality of the situation your character is in.

What do you want?

You can look at your life as being made up of a series of scenes. In each scene, you are working towards some kind of goal. Ask yourself what your character wants in each scene. Be as specific as you can. Then ask what your character is willing to do to reach that goal. In each scene, focus on your goal as the character to drive the scene forward.

Choosing sides

If you aren't given sides for your audition, the casting director might ask you to come with a prepared piece. An actor should always have one or two scenes picked and memorized just in case.

Most audition scenes are called *monologues*, since they are spoken by one person. Find a book of them at a bookstore or library, and choose a couple that are just right for you.

Popcorn Quiz

Who holds the Hollywood record for playing the most leading roles?

Can you relate? Try to find a monologue that involves a character who interests you, one you can relate to and truthfully portray.

Keep it short! When you are starting out, it's best to choose a short monologue. A good length for your first dramatic monologues is one or two pages each.

Mix it up. Prepare two pieces to show different parts of your personality. If the first piece is dramatic to show your serious side, the second should be comedic. If you're asked for one scene in an audition, choose the one most like the role you're auditioning for.

DIRECTOR'S NOTE

CHOICES WHEN YOU ARE CHOOSING YOUR GOAL IN A SCENE, MAKE SURE IT IS SPECIFIC AND CAN BE ACCOMPLISHED. IF YOU CHOOSE SOMETHING LIKE, "I WANT WORLD PEACE," CHANCES ARE YOU WILL NOT BE ABLE TO REACH YOUR GOAL IN ONE SCENE. MAKE IT AN ACTIVE GOAL (THAT'S WHY THE CRAFT IS CALLED ACT-ING). CHOOSE A GOAL THAT MOTIVATES YOU TO MOVE FORWARD INTO ACTION, LIKE WANTING TO MAKE A NEW FRIEND.

Just Before the Audition

Are you ready? You have your sides in your hand, with your lines highlighted. You've tucked your picture and resumé in your backpack, in case the casting director needs them. Now all there is to do is go to the waiting room outside the casting office, sign in, and wait for your name to be called . . .

Don't worry

It's hard not to get nervous while you're waiting to audition. You want to ask yourself questions like "What if I forget my lines?" and "What if I don't do well?" But that will only add to the tension. Bring a book to read, or some homework. Try to get your mind off how nervous you are. The best way to calm your nerves is to know that you are well prepared. Review your lines and go back over your notes, concentrating on the character and not yourself. Keep everything in the first person, saying "I" as if you already are the character.

Hi, I'm Dustin

Johnny is well prepared for his audition for *The Mists of Time*. He spent a lot of time getting a fix on the character of Dustin. Here are the notes he prepared for his audition:

My name is Dustin Wright and I turned 14 two months ago. I'm in the ninth grade and I guess my marks are OK. My teachers say I would do better if I concentrated, but I'd rather be out solving a mystery than sitting in class. I like to make up wild stories about everyday events and people. Some people say I have way too much energy and an overactive imagination. I just think I'm really creative! I have curly red hair and freckles, and I almost always wear sneakers, jeans and a T-shirt. I love reading mystery novels — Sherlock Holmes is totally my hero. I'm really close to my mother — she's pretty cool. But my younger sister Marcy gets on my nerves because she's such a "tag-along." We've always lived in small towns and this is the first time my family has moved to a city. I've made some friends, but it's been a little tough adjusting to a new place. This scene is set on a Friday afternoon in September, two weeks after the school year started. I'm on a stupid, boring tour with Marcy at the museum where Mom works. My first goal in the scene is to get away from the tour. I'll try to accomplish that by getting Marcy to leave me alone, and then sneaking off when she's not looking!

It's cold — don't freeze!

If you don't get the sides until you arrive at the audition, you have to do what's called a *cold read*, a reading you haven't prepared for in advance. The trick is to be comfortable with material you don't know very well. Don't read your lines straight off the page with your head down, because the casting director needs to be able to see your eyes. Read the sides. Find a goal quickly. What do I want? Break down the scene into "beats" or bite-sized chunks.

In the audition room, hold your sides down in front of you. Glance down at your first line, look up, deliver your line. Listen to the next line coming back at you, then look down for your next line. Don't try to find your line until it's time to say it. Just worry about one line at a time. If you get lost on the page, take a moment, find your place and keep going. Don't ask to start again. You can practice this technique of looking down and grabbing a line quickly, and looking up before delivering it. Do it at home with a book or magazine. Try it with a friend, or in front of the mirror, to make sure you can keep eye contact.

Popcorn Quiz

How old was the youngest performer to receive star billing in a movie?

DIRECTOR'S NOTE

DRESS THE PART YOU DON'T HAVE TO BUY OR WEAR ANYTHING EXTRAVAGANT OR EXPENSIVE. SOMETHING AS SIMPLE AS A CERTAIN PAIR OF SHOES OR A UNIQUE SHIRT CAN HELP YOU AND THE CASTING DIRECTOR START TO IMAGINE THAT YOU'RE LIKE THE CHARACTER. IF YOU WEAR A HAT, MAKE SURE IT DOESN'T COVER YOUR EYES — YOUR EYES ARE EXPRESSIVE, SO LET THE CASTING DIRECTOR SEE THEM.

The Audition

Suddenly, your name is called. Leave your coat, hat, boots and large bags outside the casting office. Take in your sides and your picture and resumé. Walk right in!

Introducing . . . you!

Your audition will probably start with introductions. You'll meet the casting director, and maybe the producer and director. Be sure to make eye contact! Don't be afraid to ask questions about the script or the character you're auditioning for. And answer their questions with a smile. Give them the chance to know you — the best, most enthusiastic you.

If you are tempted to answer a question with just one word — like "No" — try to remember "No, but . . . . " It keeps the conversation going, and shows that you are positive. For example, if you are asked if you like tennis and you don't, you can say, "Not really, but I love playing soccer!"

On your mark

The audition might be videotaped, so the director can play it back again later. They will show you where to take your *mark*, that is, where to stand so that you will be in the camera's frame. Be careful not to move out of the camera's boundaries.

Even if you've fully memorized your lines, you should have your sides with you. Hold them down in front of you, out of the camera frame but close enough that you can look down to get your lines quickly and then lift your head to read.

DIRECTOR'S NOTE

RIGHT OR WRONG? IN AN AUDITION, DON'T WORRY ABOUT THE CHOICES YOU MADE WHILE PREPARING. IF YOU'VE CHOSEN A GOAL THAT CAN BE ACHIEVED IN A SCENE, COMMIT YOURSELF 100% TO THAT CHOICE AND REALLY LISTEN TO THE OTHER PERSON, YOU WILL DO FINE. IF THE DIRECTOR WANTS YOU TO TRY ANOTHER GOAL, HE OR SHE WILL SUGGEST IT AFTER YOU'VE READ.

Clean slate

For the audition videotape, you will have to make a *slate*, some information to identify yourself: your name, age and height, and the name of your agent. Say this right into the camera. Speak clearly, pronounce your words well, and be energetic right off the top.

Eyes up

When you read for the role, there will probably be someone sitting just to the side of the camera. This person will read the other lines in the scene. Make and keep eye contact with this reader.

Improv your chances

Sometimes the casting director will ask you to read *off book*, to improvise. Improvising is creating a scene as you play it, without a script. Ask yourself "Who am I? What am I doing? What do I want?" Then, with the answers you've decided on, let your creativity flow.

You'll probably be improvising with someone else, so make it easy for them to advance the scene with you. Don't stop them by saying "I don't know" or "No." The two of you have to keep the scenes flowing, like jugglers have to keep balls in the air. Be open to what's coming your way.

Selection time

Casting directors look to see that you suit the character, maintain eye contact, listen, follow direction well, focus and concentrate. They want to know that you're enthusiastic about the project, and will be professional on the set.

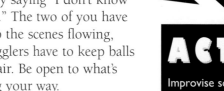

ACTION!

Improvise some scenes with a friend.

AT THE STORE • One of you plays a store clerk confronting the other, who has tried to shoplift an expensive item.

IN THE CLASSROOM • One of you plays a student trying to cheat off the other's math exam. Remember, the teacher's listening!

MAKE UP YOUR OWN characters and scenes. Play each scene out until there's a definite sense of an ending.

Popcorn Quiz

Who was one of the most famous young performers of all time?

Callback

If the producer and director want to see you again, you will get a *callback*. A callback might be to test you with other actors to see if you're a good match. Or you might be given another direction or motivation for your role, to see if you can change or strengthen something from the first audition.

Johnny's nightmare audition

1 The first audition I ever went on was a real disaster! I did everything wrong. Let me tell you about it. I had been given the script pages days in advance, but I didn't take the time to study them.

2 I was all dressed up and felt uncomfortable in my good clothes. When I noticed the rest of the kids waiting to audition dressed in everyday clothing, I remembered the character I was auditioning for was a regular kid.

3 I was really nervous waiting outside the casting office. My heart was pounding. I was sweating all over my script — I hadn't photocopied it from the fax paper, so it was smudging and I could hardly read it.

4 It was kind of awkward trying to carry my coat, boots and bag into the casting office. I stumbled, dropped my pages and almost knocked over a chair. My boots went crashing to the floor and I almost choked on my chewing gum.

5 There were three people there. I avoided meeting their eyes and answering their questions. They told me to stand in front of the camera and asked me to identify myself to start the tape. I nervously mumbled my name, my age, my height and the name of my agent.

6 In the audition, I kept my eyes on the pages and read the lines word for word. A couple of times I fumbled because I lost my place. When that happened, I lifted the pages so they came into the camera frame.

 The casting director told me that my delivery was flat. All they saw on the tape was the top of my head. Of course, I didn't get the part. My parents signed me up for audition classes, and I learned how to . . .

Ace an audition

1 For the audition for *The Mists of Time*, I'm ready. I got the script pages in lots of time, so I studied them. I feel I know the character Dustin, his goals and his relationships with the other characters.

2 I'm dressed the way I think Dustin would dress. I have my script pages in my hand, with my lines highlighted. I have my photo and resumé tucked in my backpack, just in case the casting director needs them.

3 While waiting outside the casting office, I go over my lines and review my notes. I'm nervous, but going over what I have already prepared calms me down a bit.

4 In the casting office, I'm introduced to the casting director, and I shake his hand. Two other people, the producer and director, ask me some questions. As I answer, I look right at them and let them see the real me — the perfect kid to play the part!

5 I stand up straight in front of the camera, and remind myself not to sway out of its boundaries. They ask me to identify myself in a slate, so I speak clearly and with energy, looking right into the camera.

6 I know my lines pretty well, but I hold my script pages just out of the camera frame. While I read for the part, I make sure to keep eye contact with the reader sitting to the side of the camera, and say all my lines to her.

 I thank the casting director and leave. I feel really good about the audition. All I can do now is wait and see if I get a callback . . .

You're It!

Johnny is called back to read with another actor named Charlotte. The director thought the two of them look kind of similar and could play the brother and sister in *The Mists of Time*.

Book 'em!

In the callback, the director looks for many of the same things as in the first audition. But this time she watches both actors and asks herself these questions: Do they have chemistry? Are they listening to each other? Do they play well off each other? Are they natural? Do they suit the parts? Are they focused?

The answers must be "Yes!" Johnny and Charlotte are picked to play Dustin and Marcy in *The Mists of Time*!

Charlotte is about the same age as Johnny (and looks younger), but she has already had four years of experience acting on stage and screen. It's a good chance for Johnny to pick up some tips from someone who has done this before.

26

Meanwhile . . .

While the auditions are being held and the roles are being cast, pre-production continues.

The initial idea for *The Mists of Time* came from the producer, but now it's up to the director to communicate the vision of the movie to the whole crew. The production manager is responsible for finding and hiring the crew.

There are people tracking down and managing *locations*, real places used as settings instead of sets built on a sound stage. A production designer is creating a certain "look" for the movie, planning sets and costumes. A wardrobe department starts creating the costumes. People are hired to build and light the sets. The people in the props department start collecting and building the *props* — small objects that are used on screen. There are special effects to be planned and created. Thousands of decisions are made in pre-production, and each one will affect the overall look and feel of the movie.

DIRECTOR'S NOTE

GUM? NOT! NEVER CHEW GUM IN A SCENE UNLESS THE DIRECTOR SPECIFICALLY ASKS YOU TO. IT'S HARD TO HEAR WHAT THE ACTOR IS SAYING IF HE OR SHE IS CHOMPING AWAY ON A BIG WAD OF GUM!

Charlotte speaks

"We should be getting our shooting schedules in the mail . . . and you will love craft services. Now I'm wondering if this will be mostly an exterior shoot or maybe they will blue screen all the stuff where we go back in time. What do you think?"

Charlotte might be speaking another language, for all Johnny can figure out! He asks her to slow down and take it step by step. He has a lot to learn in the upcoming weeks.

Popcorn Quiz

Who was the oldest actor to play a major role in a movie?

27

SCREEN SPEAK

costume designer
A costume designer decides what each character will wear and designs the clothes

crew
A crew is the group of people who work together to make a TV show or commercial, or a movie.

Hollywood
A place in Los Angeles, California, that used to be the movie capital of the world. The term is still used to indicate the movie business, even though many films are now shot all around the world.

production designer
The production designer creates and coordinates the visual aspects of a film or TV program: what the set looks like, where the scene is set, what an actor is holding or wearing or sitting on, etc.

production manager
This is the person responsible for keeping track of where the money is being spent on a film or TV project. The production manager advises the producer on the most economical way to spend the money so the project doesn't cost more than the budget allows.

shoot
The process of filming a TV show or commercial, or a movie.

sides
These are the pages of script or screenplay an actor uses to prepare for an audition.

wardrobe
This department is responsible for designing and creating all the costumes, and making sure they fit the actors.

SHOOT!

Production is the stage when the movie is put on film, or shot.

Trick Shots

Before shooting begins, there are a couple of tricky things you should know about the way a movie is made.

SHOOTING SCHEDULE		
Day one	*Day two*	*Day three*
scene 1	scene 10	scene 4
Int. museum	Ext. house	the schoolyard
scene 7	scene 12	
Int. museum	Ext. house	

Out of order

The director usually doesn't shoot the scenes of a movie in the same order the screenplay presents them in. Take a look at the shooting schedule for *The Mists of Time* above. Notice how scenes one and seven are shot back to back on the first day. Why? The answer is right there — whenever possible scenes at the same location are shot on the same day. It's easier to finish everything off at one location before moving the cast, crew, props, lights, trucks and everything on to the next location.

Look at Johnny's script and see what happens in scene one — Dustin leaves the tour, and he and Marcy find the coin. In scene seven, Dustin and Marcy have been sent back in time, and now return to the museum in the present. In the first scene Dustin is bored, but by the seventh he's excited because he's been on an adventure in the past. Remember the character arc (page 9)? This is a good example. To play the scenes back to back, Johnny has to know the character and the story well.

SCENE 2
TAKE 58

𝒯ake and take again

The second tricky thing is that the director will shoot several variations of the same scene. Each variation of the same scene is called a *take*.

For example, here's scene two, in which Dustin makes the world's biggest sandwich in the kitchen of his house. First there's the *master shot*, show-ing everything in the camera frame, the kitchen sink and all. The director will probably call for more than one take of this shot, to get it just right.

Next, the director wants to go in for a *close up* of the same scene. She wants to film the same shot showing just Johnny's hands and the sand-wich. So Johnny has to do exactly the same thing again.

To get the whole scene pieced together smoothly, the action from the close up has to be matched to the action from the master shot. It's important for Johnny to repeat his actions from the master shot exactly the same for the close up. Someone called a continuity person is on the set to help him remember. But it's best if Johnny pays attention to his actions in every scene.

ACTION!

GET CLOSE • A movie camera is like a spy. Stand nose to nose with a friend or family member. Are you so close you see just their eyes and nothing else? Probably not. But that's how close a camera gets shooting a close up!

Popcorn Quiz

Who invented the movie camera? When?

Countdown to Shooting

Johnny thought that once he had prepared for and aced the audition, the hard work was over. Not so fast! Preparing for his role in a movie is a lot like preparing for his audition — but on a much larger scale.

Déjà vu . . . again

The first thing Johnny does when he receives the full script is highlight all his lines. Then he starts memorizing them. This time, he memorizes them fully, because he won't have the script pages with him during filming. And he does the listening exercise with a partner. Does all this sound familiar?

Detective work

The Mists of Time is a mystery movie, but actors investigate their characters for any movie. If you're not sure about things in the screenplay — especially if it takes place in a different time or place from where you live — do some research (see *Action*, opposite). Let's say you are cast in a movie about Sherlock Holmes. How would you find out about this famous detective, the time and place he lived, and the way people looked and acted then?

Hit the books

A writer named Arthur Conan Doyle wrote short stories and books about this mystery-solving character at the end of the last century. You might read the books, or look for some of the many movies and television shows that have been based on the Sherlock Holmes stories. The stories are set in England, and Queen Victoria ruled that country at that time, so you would want to find out as much as you could about Victorian England. You might go to a library or museum to do that.

Text/subtext

What we say and what we mean can be different things. The feelings and meanings underneath what we say is called the *subtext*. Subtext can depend on where and how the character lives. So research can help the actor discover the subtext to know how to play the character well.

One week to go

It's one week before *The Mists of Time* is going to start shooting. Here's Johnny's checklist:

- ❏ Lines memorized
- ❏ Listening exercise done
- ❏ Research done
- ❏ Scene-by-scene questions answered
- ❏ Subtext established
- ❏ Character arc established

Now it's time for Johnny's wardrobe fitting. The costume designer checks to make sure the clothes chosen for his character fit.

Alterations are made to the ones that don't fit.

Finally, Johnny goes for a line reading. The entire cast gets together with the director and practices reading through the script. The line reading is the perfect time for Johnny to ask the director any questions he still has about the screenplay story or his character.

ACTION!

What if the character you are playing in the Sherlock Holmes movie is an explorer who has just come back from South America? How would you find out how to play that character?

READ • Go to the library and find books about that time period, South America and what traveling there would have been like. Don't forget that pictures might help.

SURF • If you have access to the Internet or CD-ROMs, use them to find out more.

ASK QUESTIONS • Do you know people who have been to South America? Talk to them to fill in your picture of what your character might be like.

Popcorn Quiz

What character is most often portrayed on screen?

Start Shooting

The big day has arrived! On the first day of principal photography for *The Mists of Time* the whole crew shows up and the cameras roll for the first time. Johnny arrives on the set at 7:00 a.m. to find it full of busy activity . . .

Meet the crew

The craft services table comes out, with loads of delicious food on it to feed the hungry cast and crew.

The director consults with the director of photography, also called the DP or DOP. The DP is responsible for turning the director's vision into a series of moving images. The DP chooses the type of film and lights to be used and the position of the cameras for each shot. That's

why the DP is usually the one sitting behind the camera.

The person responsible for the lighting of a shot is the gaffer. With input from the DP, the gaffer decides the most effective way to set the lights. The lights are put in place by the best boy, the gaffer's assistant.

Grips move around heavy cameras and equipment, and the key grip is the head of that group. If cameras or other equipment need to be moved or repaired, the key grip sees that it's done.

The set decorator takes direction from the production designer, placing objects and furniture on the set to make the scene look real. Properties or props are kept track of by the property manager, who makes sure they're where they need to be.

The makeup and wardrobe people are busy making the actors look like the characters they're playing. Makeup and wardrobe take polaroid pictures of the actors between scenes as reminders of exactly how an actor looks, just in case the director wants to reshoot a scene.

The script supervisor ensures continuity — that everything matches from scene to scene. An assistant director maintains order on the set and makes sure everything runs on schedule.

Cast on

The crew is busy setting the scene for the actors to step in and bring the story to life. In addition to the actors playing large roles (like Johnny), there are actors in supporting roles and stand-ins to replace the actors when the director sets up a shot. There are extras to play non-speaking background roles, and there are trained and experienced stunt doubles to safely replace the actors in action shots that could endanger the actors.

Popcorn Quiz

What was the largest number of cameras used on a film?

DIRECTOR'S NOTE

BE PREPARED MAKING MOVIES INVOLVES A LOT OF PEOPLE AND COSTS A LOT OF MONEY. ACTORS MIGHT BE THE ONES ON THE SCREEN, BUT IT TAKES THE HARD WORK OF A PROFESSIONAL CREW TO PUT THEM THERE. BE READY TO PLAY YOUR PART FROM THE FIRST DAY OF SHOOTING, SO YOU WON'T SLOW DOWN THE WHOLE PROCESS.

A Real Character

No matter how well an actor captures a character, there are people there to help. By creating makeup, or by performing stunts that the actor can't do, they contribute to how well the actor steps into the character's shoes . . . .

Talking to Jane Byrne Stevenson
makeup artist

Q: How drastically can you change the way a person looks?
A: I can go from caveman to space explorer and anything in between. I can change a person from being absolutely gorgeous to looking dreadful, or take a human being and make them look like an alien. All with makeup.
Q: Where do you get your ideas from?
A: It's not just my ideas . . . I get inspiration from the script, the director and the performers. And I rely heavily on the research I do.
Q: Do you like your job?
A: I love it! It's hard to explain — I paint on the actors like they are canvas and add to the creation of a scene. It's great!

Making it up

Your favorite action-hero's suntan; the scars of a burn victim; the over-sized head and bug-eyes of a space alien — what's the connection? If you guessed makeup, you've got it on the nose! Whether it's a natural look that takes a half-hour to apply, or complicated *special effects makeup* that takes hours to

do, movie makeup helps to create a character and add to the illusion. The camera gets very close, so makeup has to draw a very detailed picture of the character. When you see a close-up of an actor's face on a big movie screen, how big is the character's mouth?

The face of history

For a movie like *The Mists of Time*, the makeup artist has to make the actors look like people from the distant past. So the first step might be to look at mosaics and paintings that show what kind of makeup people wore. Camera tests check how the makeup will look under the bright lights used for filming. The actors might feel like they are wearing a lot of makeup, but the intense lights wash out the colors on their faces. In fact, before color film was used in movies and television, face makeup had a greenish tinge to look like realistic skin-tone in black and white!

Super stunts

What's a stunt? It's action called for in the screenplay that has to be planned, and that might not be performed by the actor playing the character. Maybe it's risky, or it may be something that requires a special skill, like driving a motorcycle or horseback riding, that the actor doesn't know how to do. A stunt coordinator takes notes from the director then designs the stunt. He or she will figure out how a stunt will be done, and will choose stunt performers to work on a particular film or television show.

Double dare

Stunt doubles take the places of actors in scenes that might be dangerous. Some scenes might call for stunt work without doubling.

Stunt work is dangerous, and fear is fear, right? Not exactly. There are different types of fear — good and bad. If fear is under control, it makes stunt people centered, so they can do whatever they have to do. But if a stunt double is scared because there's a chance of getting hurt, there's probably something wrong with the way the stunt is designed. Solid preparation is the key.

Popcorn Quiz

What deadly ingredient was used in popular face cosmetics in 18th-century Europe?

DIRECTOR'S NOTE

SENSES IT'S NOT ENOUGH TO LOOK LIKE A CHARACTER — YOU HAVE TO BE SENSITIVE TO HOW THE CHARACTER FEELS. EXPERIENCE LIFE WITH ALL YOUR SENSES: SIGHT, SOUND, SMELL, TOUCH AND TASTE. PAY CLOSE ATTENTION TO YOUR SENSES AND PUT THE FEELINGS IN A "SENSE MEMORY" FILE IN YOUR HEAD. WHEN YOU'RE CALLED UPON TO ACT OUT CERTAIN RESPONSES, YOU CAN OPEN THAT FILE AND USE YOUR MEMORIES TO RE-CREATE A REALISTIC RESPONSE.

Talking to Alison Reid
stunt double

Q: What are some of the stunts you've done?
A: I've rolled cars. I've done stair falls and high jumps. And I've been set on fire.
Q: Any advice for someone who wants to do stunts?
A: Think about it very carefully. Chances are, sooner or later, you're going to get hurt. If you've thought about it a lot, and still want to do it, then train in sports. Try to develop as many skills as you can — horseback riding, driving a motorcycle, climbing, etc. See if you can get on a job as an extra for a movie or television show, so you can observe set etiquette, how things are run.

The Shoot

From Johnny's journal

Day One: 9:00 a.m. Well, here we are . . . first day on the set and I'm kind of nervous. I spent the first half hour of the day in my trailer doing breathing exercises and working on my goal for the first scene. Yes, I do have a trailer, and it's sort of like the one my family uses when we go camping for summer holidays.

9:30 a.m. Look at me — having makeup put on! I hope this picture doesn't get around school. The director came in to tell us that we'll be shooting scene seven before scene one. I am going to spend a few minutes reviewing the scene so I can remember what my character is doing and what my goal is in scene seven.

10:00 a.m. Just about to shoot the master shot. I'm glad the wardrobe people are taking these polaroids or we wouldn't be able to remember exactly how to dress me and make me up again. Gotta get those funny overalls just right!

1:00 p.m. Time for lunch! The first scene is "in the can" — a movie-making term for "it's been shot." It wasn't as tough as I imagined. I just paid attention, focused on what the director was saying, concentrated and listened to what Charlotte was saying as Marcy in the scenes. I'm really glad I prepared beforehand. P.S. We had spaghetti for lunch — my fave!

From Charlotte's diary

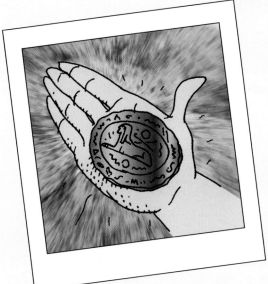

ACTION!

AS IF • It's hard to put yourself into a scene if you've never had the experience your character has. For example, what if you have to break down crying because your chimpanzee friend has died? You've probably never had a chimp as a friend. But you can imagine something very close to the experience and replace it in your imagination. If you have a pet dog, react as if your dog was the chimpanzee that had just died.

Day Five

Of all the movie shoots I've been on, I think this one is the most fun yet! I really like Johnny — he's great to work with, even though he's never acted in a movie before. Here's a picture of the coin our characters find. It's sort of like our good luck charm. W e are supposed to finish shooting in 10 more days — I can't believe we're that far along the shooting schedule already. So much is happening that it's going by really fast.

    Today Johnny asked my advice. He was having a hard time understanding how his character, Dustin, would feel in a scene where he wakes up from a bad nightmare. He said he'd never had a nightmare — can you believe it?! I told him about an exercise called "As If." I learned it from a director once.

Popcorn Quiz

What was the longest film ever made?

Film School

There's nothing like learning from experience! Once *The Mists of Time* starts shooting, Johnny sees all kinds of things in action that help him understand the process better . . .

Acute angles

On set, the director and camera operator discuss all the different camera angles for each shot.

The master shot is a camera angle that is fairly wide, and it usually has all the actors from the scene included in the frame.

A medium shot is a little closer, but not too close.

Takes time . . .

Making movies can be a slow process. Before the director shoots a scene, the stage has to be set to look real. That starts with picking or building a location — for *The Mists of Time*, it's a museum. Next comes dressing the area by putting props — ancient-looking pottery and art — in the space. Finally, the set is lit so it shows up well on camera.

Then the director has to *block out* the scene. That means she has the actors rehearse the scene right in the set.

Every scene will be shot more than once. Usually the master shot of a scene is filmed first. Then the camera is moved to set up for a medium shot. The actors will get close-up shots, and the director will choose the ones to use later. Last up is the filming of extreme close-ups or *cutaways*. These are the really close-up shots of hands picking up things and other important details.

When it's time to shoot the director calls, "Rolling!" so the cast and crew know the camera is getting started and that the scene will begin in a few seconds. "Action!" is the cue that it's time for the scene to begin. Once a scene is finished, the director will say, "Cut!" If the director likes any part of the scene that was just shot, she will call out, "Cut and print!" so the scene will be sent to the lab to be developed. It takes time to print a film, but a special lab can make a quick, rough print of film scenes called *rushes*.

Whew! A lot goes into shooting a scene. Sometimes the cast and crew shoot all day and only film one or two pages of screenplay. But that's show business!

Popcorn Quiz
What is an Oscar?

And overtime

Even after shooting is done for the day, the work isn't. The director and crew are watching the rushes to make sure they are getting what they need on film. The location manager confirms the location for the next day's shooting.

The director and screenwriter might update and rewrite scenes right up to the shooting day. How does everyone tell the old scenes from the new? The updated pages are printed on paper of a different color. The old pages are pulled out and in go the pages in that day's color.

The Mists of Time is shooting over summer break, so Johnny and Charlotte don't have to study between scenes. During the school year, a tutor makes sure that young actors don't fall behind in their studies.

For a close-up, the camera moves in to capture an actor's action from a very short distance.

The extreme close-up, or cutaway, is so close, all you can see are the actor's eyes, or whatever the director chooses to highlight.

DIRECTOR'S NOTE

MAKE IT IMPORTANT ONE OF THE KEYS TO PLAYING A SCENE WELL IS MAKING SURE THE GOALS YOU SET FOR YOURSELF ARE IMPORTANT TO YOU. IF YOU DON'T CARE ABOUT YOUR CHARACTER, YOUR GOAL OR YOUR RELATIONSHIP TO THE OTHER PERSON IN THE SCENE, IT WILL SHOW ON THE SCREEN. IF YOU'RE NOT INTERESTED AND ENGAGED, THE AUDIENCE WILL BE BORED. IF YOU CARE, THEY WILL.

☆ Causin' Effects

Movie-making is like magic, and some things created for the screen are truly spectacular. Special effects, or SFX, and visual effects make the impossible seem real.

Talking to Eric Brevig

special effects artist

Q: What's the neatest special effect you've ever created?

A: That's a hard one. Let me think . . . I don't think there is just one. I think some of the work I helped create for the movie *The Abyss* was a lot of fun. We filmed pieces of scenes 50 feet (17 m) underwater and then made it seem like the actors were beside a sunken submarine. In fact, the sub was shot on a smoke-filled stage, and then matched with the underwater shots months later. And in the movie *Total Recall*, there's a scene where Arnold Schwarzenegger is traveling in a train and the camera is flying along looking in a window at him. The camera pulls back to reveal this incredible Martian landscape. Once again, we shot the train sequence on a modest interior sound stage in Mexico. The landscape was created in a miniature motion control stage in California. It was matched up later in post-production.

Seeing things

Sometimes, what a director visualizes is rare or even impossible — that's where *effects* come in. The screenplay describes what the director wants the audience to see. A special effects artist draws up a *storyboard* to illustrate the process step by step. Although most people call all effects *special effects*, a special effect is performed and shot on the set. A *visual effect* is created either with the camera itself, or it's done after shooting in post-production. Fantasy shots and scenes that might endanger actors are usually done with computers.

Let's fly!

How do you make a superhero fly? Until about 20 years ago, you'd film her hanging on wires in front of a screen with a picture of the sky on it. Now, film of her on wires in front of a special blue screen is combined with other film (see opposite). This process used to be limited by how precisely the camera could be moved, but now computers help control the camera. Also, images can be programmed into a computer and moved around in three dimensions. The actor can fly without her feet ever leaving the ground!

How to walk through walls

In *The Mists of Time*, Marcy and Dustin pass through the museum wall to go back in time. How would a special effects artist make this look real? There are a couple of ways it could be done.

Special effects are handled "on the floor" as part of the shoot. This scene would be shot with the camera angled to the side. The actors walk through an opening in the wall that is cleverly hidden by the angle of the shot. For other scenes, the opening would be filled in. It's like a magic trick — now you see it, now you don't!

But what if we wanted to see the actors actually *penetrating* the wall? That would take more than a special effect. As an elaborate visual effect, it would involve shooting different parts of what we see, and putting them together in post-production. It would work like this . . .

Popcorn Quiz

When was the first "smellie" released?

Getting visual

1 This visual effect is called "blue screening" because a blue screen is shot and then everything blue is replaced later on. The trick is to film the actors and the wall separately. First, the director shoots the wall without any actors. This is used as the background shot.

2 Next, the foreground shot is taken. The actors stand in front of a blue screen that represents the wall. They press their hands and bodies against the screen as though they're passing right into the wall. The scene is filmed from several angles, and the actors have to react as if they were going through the wall.

3 The director combines the two images in post-production. Everything blue is made to disappear from the image. Computers are used to animate or distort the surface of the wall so it reacts to the actors' hands. What you see on screen is an image of the actors pushing through the wall.

SCREEN SPEAK

assistant director
Assistant directors maintain order on the set and make sure everything runs on schedule.

best boy
As the gaffer's assistant, a best boy does the physical lifting and placing of lights on the set.

boom operator
The boom operator holds up a microphone on a long stick and places it just above the actors but out of camera range to record the actors' dialogue

camera operator assistants
These people make sure that the camera is in focus and film is always loaded efficiently without disrupting the flow of shooting.

continuity person
This person is responsible for keeping track of all the details during the shooting of a film. This includes the number and length of each take, the dialogue, the movement and the position of characters and props in a scene. The continuity person ensures each take of the same shot matches the rest.

craft services
The craft services team keeps the cast and crew fed on the set.

director of photography
Also known as the DP or DOP, the director of photography turns the director's vision into a series of moving images.

gaffer
The gaffer decides the best way to place the lights and is responsible for the lighting of a shot.

key grip
The key grip is in charge of the lifting and fixing of equipment, such as cameras. A key grip also solves technical problems as they crop up on the set.

makeup artist
This person applies the makeup to the actors in a film, to make them look attractive, or to change the way they look altogether.

property manager
In charge of all properties or props, the property manager makes sure that objects used in scenes don't break or disappear from the set.

set decorator
The set decorator places objects such as furniture on a set to make it look realistic.

sound mixer
The sound mixer monitors the levels of the audio signal as the actors' voices are being recorded.

special effects artist
Special effects artists create extraordinary or unusual images for the camera.

stand-in
A stand-in substitutes for an actor while the director sets up a shot.

stunt coordinator
A stunt coordinator plans stunts and chooses the stunt doubles to perform them.

stunt double
A stunt double is a trained professional who substitutes for an actor to perform a dangerous or difficult action.

visual effects team
These people work after the film has been shot to create effects using computers and other digital means. They are responsible for the effects that can't be executed on the set.

PUZZLE PIECES

The film is pieced together and all the effects and sounds are added in post-production.

Piecing It All Together

After the shoot is finished and the film is developed, what does it look like? A bunch of bits and pieces, scenes and parts of scenes, that must be put together. So it's off to an editing suite, where a film editor sits at a computer or a machine called a Moviola and gets to work . . .

All in the edit

The process of editing can make or break a film, and it happens mostly in the mind of the editor. The film is a whole bunch of separate pieces of film. There are different angles and performances — some scenes don't even go all the way through to the end. A film editor arranges these pieces and chooses the focus for each scene.

It's a lock!

Once each scene is working, the film editor and director turn their attention to the rhythm and pace of the movie. *Continuity* is the order of the scenes. Sometimes a director might choose to mix up the the continuity, maybe put scene 34 before scene 20.

Transitions are the pieces that link the scenes together, and there are many types — straight cuts from one scene to the next, dissolves in which the picture slowly disappears to be replaced by the next image, sound cuts. When the film is seen as a whole, suddenly scenes that worked on their own are too slow or too fast, too short or too long. The scenes have to be fitted together like the pieces of a jigsaw puzzle. When the whole picture feels right to the director and the editor, then the picture is "locked."

Got it covered

An editor can do almost anything in the editing room, as long as there's enough *coverage*. Coverage is another word for the number of shots taken of the same scene. In the earlier days of film, the camera would just follow the actors from the beginning to the end of a scene. The editors wouldn't have much cutting to do. But there wasn't much coverage if they wanted to choose different angles. Now, most films have lots of coverage, and lots of film is shot. It protects the director, who will have many different angles to choose from in the editing suite.

"E" is for . . .

"E" is for editing. It's also for electronics. All film editing used to be done on a Moviola. Now editors can choose to stick with the traditional equipment or use computers.

Finally, "e" is for effects. Post-production is where some amazing visual effects can be created (see page 43 for a description of one of these effects). From walking through walls and flying, to "morphing" and disappearing, almost anything is possible if you have computers.

Talking to Michael Kahn
film editor

Q: How did you get started in film editing?
A: I had no intentions of becoming an editor. At first I didn't think I had the expertise. I was afraid. The first scene I ever cut, I was sitting with the director and all this film thinking, "What do I do? Where do I start?" Well, I just jumped right in and it worked!
Q: What can actors do to make your job easier?
A: The best advice I have, especially for young actors, is to NOT look right into the camera. Also, listen to the director's instruction. Once you start the scene, you have to keep going until you hear the director yell, "Cut!" Don't stop mid-way through, even if you've flubbed a line or two. An editor could use part of that scene before or after the mistake.
Q: Does a film stay with you when you're not "at work"?
A: It NEVER leaves. The mind is a problem solver. You feed the problem in and something happens to solve it. There could be a hundred ways to put a scene together; there's lots of options, like a giant puzzle. Except the puzzle is alive! Sometimes I do puzzles at home. I'll look at the shape of a piece and see if I can place it quickly. I guess it's a spatial thing. It helps me to exercise the part of my brain that helps problem-solve in the editing suite.

Popcorn Quiz

On average, how much film ends up on the cutting room floor?

ACTION!

Continuing a scene after making a mistake takes real concentration. When it comes to concentration, practice makes perfect.

1 • Draw a big circle on paper.
2 • Tape the paper to the wall at eye level.
3 • Every night, sit in front of it.
4 • Clear your mind and see how long you can stare at the circle before other thoughts pop into your mind.
5 • Gently bring your concentration back to the circle.
6 • Every night, spend a little longer in front of the circle. Soon you will see that you can focus your thoughts quickly and easily.

Did You Hear?

When movies were first invented, they didn't have sound. The actors' dialogue would appear written on the screen, and the movie theater would have someone playing music to go with the film. But, with the start of talking films, or "talkies," suddenly actors could speak for themselves . . .

Say that again

When dialogue recorded during shooting doesn't come through clearly, it's replaced later in ADR, or Automated Dialogue Replacement. ADR is tough for actors because they have to exactly match the words they are saying with what's on the film. Have you seen a movie where the way the actors' mouths move doesn't match the sounds coming out? Now you know why!

The actors stand in front of a screen, and scenes are projected onto it. The actors watch for two white lines that move across the screen and meet in the middle. When the two white lines become one, it's time for the missing line.

Do the dub!

What if *The Mists of Time* is sold to countries where other languages are spoken? Actors might be hired to *dub* the lines, or re-record them into their own language, even if the voices won't exactly match the mouth movements Johnny and Charlotte made. Sometimes, other countries use subtitles on the screen instead of dubbing the actors' voices.

Music to your ears

The last things added to the movie are background music and sound. They aren't done until the scenes are in order, and everything is in place.

The director tells a composer where he or she would like to hear music, and what kind of effect the music should make. There are two types of music in a film score: environmental music accents the physical surroundings in a film; and character-driven music evokes a particular character and hints at what that character is thinking or feeling. Once the composer writes the music, it is played by musicians and recorded. Then it gets mixed onto the soundtrack.

48

Sounds good

Finally, *sound effects* and *foley* are used to enhance the action in the movie. Sound effects are like special effects for your ears — the sounds that add to what you see onscreen.

Foley is a system named after its inventor, Jack Foley. It replaces or adds to everyday sounds in the movie. Footsteps, keys jingling, a drink with ice cubes tipping over — some sounds you don't even think about are among the things that foley artists create. Sometimes foley artists also help out with sound effects — for example, glass breaking, an explosion or a fire burning.

Foley artists use their imaginations and everyday objects to come up with just the right sound — a drum might be just the thing a foley artist needs to re-create the sound of thunder. Foley artists are responsible for all kinds of sounds, from something as small as brushing a hand across your cheek to something as big as a train wreck.

This is how it's done. The supervising sound editor for the movie makes up a "road map" of the sounds throughout the movie. Notes called cue sheets tell the foley artists what specific sounds they need to produce. Then it's off to the foley stage. The foley stage is a big, empty space with different surfaces such as dirt, cement and wood floors to walk on. And, of course, there are all the props — from a bathroom plunger to gelatin, anything can be used.

ACTION!

MAKE NOISE • Touch, tickle and shake all the objects in your room.
LISTEN • Close your eyes and listen to the sounds they make.
USE YOUR IMAGINATION • What else could each of the sounds be used for?

Popcorn Quiz

When was the first "talkie" released?

DIRECTOR'S NOTE

DON'T FAKE IT AN ACCENT, THAT IS. IF ONE IS REQUESTED IN YOUR AUDITION AND YOU'RE NOT COMFORTABLE WITH IT, DON'T EVEN TRY. IF THEY LIKE YOUR READING IN THE FIRST AUDITION, THEY MIGHT CAST YOU AND HIRE A DIALECT COACH TO HELP YOU.

SCREEN SPEAK

ADR operator
The ADR (automated dialogue replacement) operator works with actors after filming is complete, to re-record any dialogue that was unclear when it was shot.

composer
The composer writes music, or a score, to accompany the visuals in a film.

dialect coach
This person helps actors speak a foreign language or speak with a foreign accent convincingly.

dubbing
This is the process of mixing all dialogue, sound effects and music together on a single track.

editor
The editor takes all the scenes that have been shot and arranges them in the best order to tell the story in the most effective way.

foley artist
This professional specializes in making sound effects to match the actors' movements on screen.

silent film
An early movie that has no sound. Most silent films were made between 1895 and 1927.

sound editor
This person's job is to assemble and synchronize all the sounds effects and music tracks.

sound stage
A special studio for shooting and recording sound for a film or TV show. Most sound stages are designed so that sounds are crisp and clear.

talkie
A movie with sound.

TO MARKET, TO MARKET

Selling a movie is more than getting people to buy tickets to see it. First, it has to be sold to the theaters.

Super Markets

Actors won't see the final film until months after shooting is finished. But all that time is well spent. As the movie is being finished, people are getting the word out and selling it to lots of theaters.

Creating a buzz

A publicity company works hard to promote the film, to get it lots of publicity and attention. A publicist will make up packages of photos of Johnny and Charlotte in *The Mists of Time* with information about the movie, and send them to radio and TV stations, newspapers and magazines.

If the movie is sold to various markets, it will be shown in lots of different places. The team responsible for selling the film is called the distribution company. *The Mists of Time* has received *wide release*, which means that it will be shown in many movie theaters in many cities and countries around the world.

Trailers

People see a poster for an upcoming movie. Or they might hear about it through word of mouth, advertisements or interviews in magazines, radio and television. But one of the best ways to get the public interested in the movie's upcoming release is through a trailer. This isn't the kind of trailer that's pulled by a truck. A movie trailer is a collection of scenes or *clips* from the movie. It's a commercial for the film that shows the highlights and tries to entice people to see it. You've probably seen trailers on TV or the last time you went to a movie.

Meet the press

About a week before *The Mists of Time* opens, the publicist sets up times for the press to interview Johnny and Charlotte. Charlotte had done press interviews for television, radio and magazines, and she had a few good tips for Johnny. Here they are, to the right:

Popcorn Quiz

Who are
the most successful
producer/directors in
terms of box-office
money?

1 Remember to ask the publicist for a press kit before you do the interview. The press kit contains a lot of written information about the film, and it will be a good source of details for you.

2 Spit out your gum before doing an interview. I forgot to do that for a TV interview, and you could hear me chomping all the way through the tape!

3 Speak every word distinctly, and try not to talk a million miles an hour. Slow and clear is best.

4 Be careful that you don't pass on any negative information. It's like gossiping, it's bad for the film, and it's definitely not professional.

5 Practice using short, snappy sentences to describe the plot of the movie. Don't ramble on, and save some mystery for the people to see on screen. Don't give away the ending!

6 Watch entertainment shows and read interviews in magazines. Which actors do you think come off sounding good? How do they make you want to see their movies? Learn from them.

☆ You on the Big Screen

Just before a new movie is released to the public, the cast and crew get to see it. What's it like to see yourself on a screen for the first time? How does it feel to read a review of a movie you're in? And what about when it's all over?

"It's really cool . . ."

Some young actors share their feelings about seeing themselves onscreen:

The first time I saw myself on film, it was a really odd feeling. To this day I still feel a little uneasy when watching my work — I almost feel like I'm under a microscope.

— *Laura Bertram*

The first time I saw myself on TV, it seemed surreal. It didn't even feel like it was me.

— *Lani Billard*

I was really happy. It was fun to see myself on television and I always called my parents to come running to the family room when my commercial was on TV.

— *Marc Donato*

It's really cool. Every time I heard my line, I went, "Look! I got a line! I got a line!"

— *Graham Losee*

Work review

After a movie is released to the public, a movie review might appear. A movie critic decides what he or she liked or disliked about a movie, and sums it up in a review. Here's a review of *The Mists of Time*:

The Mists of Time is directed by the woman who brought us *Green-Eyed Monster*. This fun-for-the-whole-family film follows two sibling rivals as they unlock a deep, dark secret from the ancient past after discovering an old coin in a museum. The brother and sister soon learn the importance of working together as they find themselves in ancient Egypt where a battle is about to begin. The two characters, Dustin and Marcy, have to move fast — and they do. Acting like super sleuths, they piece together clues that help them straighten out the course of history and save a few lives in the process.

I liked *The Mists of Time*. It's an example of time travel adventure at its best. The main characters, played by Charlotte Wright and newcomer Johnny Young, were solid and believable. My only complaint is that the middle seemed a bit flat and lacked energy. However, the film picked up, and the ending is absolutely terrific. I'd highly recommend this movie for a family outing.

Life after the movie

Let's catch up with Johnny and Charlotte a year after *The Mists of Time* has been released. They've stayed in touch with each other through e-mail.

Date: December 2 9:12 am
From: johnnyy@hillcrest.edu (Johnny Young)
To: charw@server.net (Charlotte Wright)
Subject: Hi!

Hey, you! Guess what I did last night. I rented "The Mists of Time." I laughed my head off at the part where we have to wear those toga things. We looked so goofy.:-r In answer to your question -- no, I haven't been on an audition for a while. Guess the last one was for that line of mountain bikes. I did four national commercials in a row. It was a blast! Are you taking the scene-study workshop next weekend? My agent says it'll be really good. Oh, I aced that English exam last week and I just joined the soccer team. Pretty neat, huh? A teacher asked me the other day if I'm going to drama school after I graduate. I might. But, then again, I've always thought about being a doctor. Or maybe an archaeologist? TTYL
                                                    Johnny

P.S. Maybe I'll go to film school and be a director. Wouldn't it be cool if I directed you in something someday?

Popcorn Quiz
Who invented the film projector?

Date: December 2 2:23 pm
From: charw@server.net (Charlotte Wright)
To: johnnyy@hillcrest.edu (Johnny Young)
Subject: Hi, back at ya!

Hey there, Johnny!
You're not going to believe this -- I went to a sleep-over party two nights ago, and guess what we watched. "The Mists of Time"! Of course, it was two in the morning and I was falling asleep on the couch. I picked up the pictures from the wrap party last week -- only took me a year to get them developed! There are some pretty funny shots. The one of you stuffing pasta in your mouth is very glam.;> I've been really busy -- I just shot three episodes of a series and two commercials. And I just got cast in a Movie of the Week as a daughter who has a fatal illness. A cheerful little role. Mom brought home information about a drama program in New York. It's a four-year course and it would start right after I graduate from high school. Imagine me in New York -- I'd spend all my time eating and shopping! BFN

                                                    Charlotte

P.S. Yes, I'd love to go to the scene-study class. Can you send me more information on it?

SCREEN SPEAK

box office
The place where tickets to a movie are sold. The term has come to mean how much money a film makes.

clips
Selected pieces or scenes from a film that are used to give an idea of the look or style of the movie.

distribution company
A distribution company markets films and makes arrangements to have them shown onscreen or sold through video outlets.

film critic
A film critic judges a film or TV show soon after it is released to the public and states his or her opinions of the show in a review.

publicist
The publicist is in charge of all publicity on a film or TV project.

publicity company
This group of people is hired to spread the word about a film by writing articles and press releases, and by arranging for the stars to be interviewed on radio or TV, or in magazines and newspapers.

OFF THE BIG SCREEN

Here are some auditions
actors can go on —
but not in the movies.

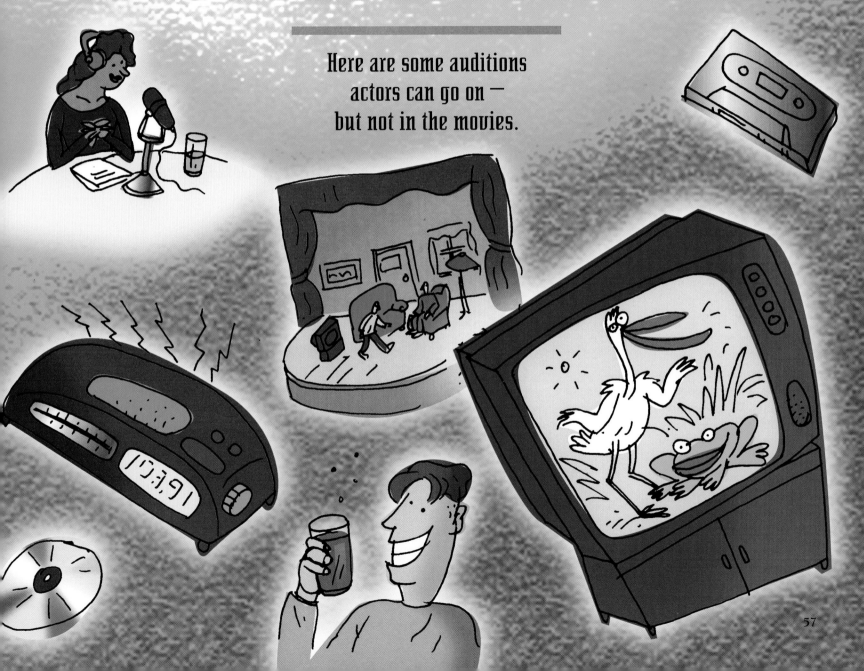

The Stage and the Small Screen

Auditioning for acting work on television or for live theater is a lot like auditioning for a movie. But there are some differences . . .

Onstage now

Acting onstage — in school plays or with a community theater group — is a great way to develop your craft.

There are two main differences between acting onstage and acting on screen. The first difference is how close your audience is. When you are being filmed, the camera is like a spy eavesdropping on your conversation. You don't speak more loudly than usual or exaggerate your actions. But when you're acting on stage, the audience can be seated pretty far away from you. You have to project your lines — that means speaking loudly and clearly enough that

you can be heard in the back row. You also have to make your movements quite large.

When you are acting for the camera, the scenes are shot out of order and several takes are shot for each scene. On stage, the play unfolds in order, and you don't have a second chance — until the next performance.

Popcorn Quiz

What is "prime time"?

58

In a series

When you audition for a role in a television series, your make-believe situation comes from a script, not a screenplay. A script for a TV show is usually a third (for a half-hour show) to a half (for an hour show) the length of a movie screenplay. The stories are generally simpler, consisting of just a couple of acts and a handful of scenes.

The producers generally shoot 13 episodes to make up a season. You could get cast in one or a few episodes. If you luck out and get a cast in a recurring role, audiences will tune in and see you on the show regularly.

Super sell

Television commercials are made to sell a product. The actor is supposed to motivate viewers to go buy whatever the sponsor wants to sell.

You might not receive a side for a commercial audition. Instead, they might ask you to give a look of joy or fear or another emotion. They want to see if you can take direction well, and if you can show your emotions. A commercial doesn't give you a lot of time to get your feelings across.

In any case, find out the product name and make sure it stands out in your reading. Find excitement for what they want you sell.

Ace a commercial audition

1 Ask yourself, "What is the product?" and "What need will it satisfy?"

2 If you don't have time to memorize your script, break it into short bits. Say your lines a few words at a time.

3 Instead of focusing to the person to the side of the camera, read into the camera (unless you are told otherwise).

4 If you don't like the product, do the "As If" exercise (page 39). If pizza is not your favorite food but you're a real chocoholic, eating it can be "as if you're eating chocolate." Imagine your best friend is on the other side of the camera lens, and your reading will be warm and friendly.

Speak Up

Here's a riddle for you: when can an actor sound like a superhero but not look like a superhero?

Talking to Alyson Court

voice-over actor

Q: How did you get into voice work?

A: When I was young I attended a drama program at the School for the Arts. I got an agent and, when I was eleven, they sent me to my first cartoon audition for the cartoon *Ewoks*. I got it!

Q: Of the cartoon characters you've played, who's your favorite?

A: Definitely the character of Lydia from *Beetlejuice*. That show was wonderful to work on. The scripts were great. Also, it was the first time my character had some real spunk. She was a very cool character.

Q: Any advice for kids out there who want to do voice work?

A: If you think this is something you'd like to do, then look into singing and projection classes in your area. Voice-over acting is enjoyable because it doesn't matter what you look like — it's simply based on talent. Oh yeah, it helps if you can read!

Disguise your voice

Did you ever think about how often you hear an actor's voice, but never see the actor? As an actor, you might get a chance to audition for radio commercials and programs, stories on tape or CD, and commercials or narrative for television. But *voice-over* work is mostly used for cartoons — animated series for TV, or even full-length movies.

When you arrive at a cartoon audition, most producers will show you a sketch of the character and an outline describing what the character is like. Sometimes there are also storyboards, which show a frame-by-frame layout of the script so you can see the action that goes along with the dialogue. And, if you're really lucky, the producers might have told your agent some of the personality traits of the character.

Be a 'toon in tune

In animation, which comes first, the voice or the pictures? Surprisingly, the cartoon doesn't get animated until the end. The actors come in first and record all the dialogue! During voice-over sessions, actors read from *line scripts*, while the producers and directors make sure the pacing of the dialogue matches the action that the animators will be drawing at a later date.

One of the hardest things about voice-overs is learning to project all your emotions through your voice. Your voice is your only way of showing who the character is. There are some technical tricks to keep in mind, too. If you're recording with someone else, you have to be careful you don't jump on their lines, or pop your "p"s, or blow into the microphone. For voice work, your "instrument" should be tuned by taking singing classes and working with a vocal coach to help you with good pronunciation and clear articulation.

Practice makes perfect

No matter where your acting takes you — onto the stage or screen, on television or on the radio for a voice-over — where you end up isn't as important as getting there. Like playing music, painting pictures or building furniture, acting is a craft you have to work on to perfect. You have to love acting and be dedicated enough to work hard if you want to learn all there is to know about it. The fact remains that very few people ever get to the point of being cast in a movie. Most people don't even get a chance to audition. But if you care about acting, the opportunity to study the craft is valuable all by itself. Studying the craft of acting has lots of benefits — it can sharpen your senses, increase your confidence, exercise your imagination and help you to learn more about yourself.

ACTION!

READ • Practice reading from a book or magazine into a tape recorder.
PLAY BACK • When you play your recordings back, really listen to yourself.
ASK • Ask yourself: Am I pronouncing my words clearly? Do I make the words come to life? Do I have a knack for accents or characterization?
LISTEN • Listen to other people's voices. Watch cartoons and listen to the voices being used.

DIRECTOR'S NOTE

ALL VOICE THE TRICKIEST THING ABOUT DOING VOICE-OVER WORK IS THAT YOU HAVE TO ACT WITHOUT USING FACIAL EXPRESSIONS OR BODY LANGUAGE. CHARACTER, EMOTION AND ACTION ALL HAVE TO BE COMMUNICATED THROUGH THE RHYTHM AND TONE OF YOUR VOICE. BE AWARE OF WHAT YOU SOUND LIKE AND HOW MUCH YOU CAN EXPRESS JUST BY CHANGING THE WAY YOU SPEAK.

SCREEN SPEAK

commercial
A short (usually 30 seconds to one minute) piece of TV video, film for theaters or tape for radio, to advertise a product or service.

film/video/tape
Film is the thin, transparent material that captures images to be projected on a screen; video is the combination of picture and sound transmitted by a TV system; tape is the medium for sound only.

line script
A script for a cartoon voice-over with just the spoken lines.

sponsor
For a TV commercial, the sponsor is the company that pays for the opportunity to promote their product or themselves.

storyboard
This is a series of sketches that illustrates action from a screenplay or TV script.

vocal coach
A vocal coach helps performers speak their lines clearly and use their voices effectively.

ANSWERS

page 5
In 1895, audiences watched a 30-second film called *L'arroseur arrose*, or "the waterer watered." A little boy, helping a gardener water flowers, puts his foot down on the hose. When the flow of water stops, the gardener peers into the hose. The boy moves his foot and the gardener gets drenched. The "little rascal" in the short film was the screen's first child actor.

page 9
John Hughes wrote the script for *Weird Science* in two days. Hughes also wrote *The Breakfast Club* in 3 days, *National Lampoon's Vacation* in 4 days and *Mr. Mom* in less than a week.

page 11
The ratio is about one minute of screen time per page of screenplay. Since the average movie runs two hours or 120 minutes, it takes approximately 120 pages of screenplay to make a movie.

page 13
More than 2,000 actors auditioned. The role went to a newcomer, a kid who had not acted in film before.

page 17
A film of the story of the Kelly Gang was made in Australia in 1906. The film was 1333 m (4000 feet) long and had a running time of between 60 and 70 minutes.

page 19
John Wayne had leading roles in 142 feature movies.

page 21
Leroy Overacker, known on screen as Baby Leroy, was six months old when he played opposite Maurice Chevalier in a movie called *Bedtime Story*.

page 23
Shirley Temple started acting and singing in movies when she was five years old. Among her movies were *Little Miss Marker*, *The Little Colonel*, *The Little Rebel*, *Captain January*, *Poor Little Rich Girl*, *Heidi* and *Rebecca of Sunnybrook Farm*. When she was the number-one box-office attraction in Hollywood, Shirley Temple was getting an allowance of $4.25 per week.

page 27
Lillian Gish was 93 when *The Whales of August* finished shooting in 1993.

page 31
Thomas Edison invented the movie camera in 1889.

page 33
Master detective Sherlock Holmes, created by Sir Arthur Conan Doyle (1859–1930), has been played by 75 actors in 211 films.

page 35
A feature-length documentary called *One Day of War* used 160 cameras.

page 37
Women used to cover their faces with lead paint to make their skin silky smooth, but there was one problem. The ingredients were toxic, and many people poisoned themselves.

page 39
The longest film ever made was *The Cure for Insomnia*, and it was 85 hours long.

page 41
Oscars are Academy Awards, presented in Hollywood by the Academy of Motion Picture Arts and Sciences. The awards honor outstanding achievements in writing, editing, acting and other film-making crafts. The figure of a man with a crusader's sword standing on a reel of film was known as the "statuette" until Academy librarian Margaret Herrick remarked that the statue looked like her Uncle Oscar, and the nickname stuck.

page 43
The feature-length *My Dream* premiered at the Swiss Pavillion of the New York World's Fair on October 10, 1940. The director of smells for the film, Hans E. Laube, claimed he could reproduce more than 4,000 odors, including flowers, forest, tea, honey, smoked meat and tar.

page 47
For an average two hour movie, between 100,000 m and 150,000 m (300,000 to 400,000 feet) of film get cut down to approximately 3500 m (10,000 feet) of final film.

page 49
The earliest talking films were presented in a Paris exposition on June 8, 1900.

page 53
George Lucas and Steven Spielberg are responsible for producing and directing 9 of the 16 films that have made more than $100 million worldwide.

page 55
Louis Lumiere invented the film projector. In his first public show in 1895, he showed a scene of a train arriving at a railway station. The audience had never seen anything like it, and flinched when they saw the steam on the screen heading towards them.

page 58
Every evening, between about 7:00 and 11:00, more people are watching television than any other time of the day. Since these times attract more viewers, TV stations put on the shows with the best chances of success during the prime time.

page 61
A three-minute cartoon sequence in *The King of Jazz* made by Walter Lanz was in two-color technicolor. It depicted a bandleader on a big-game hunt in Africa.

A NOTE TO PARENTS

If your child announces that he or she would like to act professionally in films or for television, there are a few things you should know. The business of show business is, first and foremost, a business. It can be very exciting, but it requires commitment from both child and parent.

If you research and find a good agent, that agent will try to arrange auditions for your child. The auditions usually take place after school hours; however, someone will have to transport the actor to and from the audition location.

If a child gets cast in a role, dedication is required from both actor and parent. In most cases, rules are in place that a chaperone must be present on the set for the whole time the child is working. If a parent cannot be the chaperone, someone else must be appointed. All chaperones must sign a form agreeing to their duties in watching out for the child actor's safety and best interests.

It's no secret that the world of acting can be a fickle place. It's extremely important that parents be very supportive of their children. They should reassure children that, even if they don't get cast in roles, their pursuit of excellence in this or any craft is the real goal. A child's self-confidence is more valuable than any role.

Remember that you shouldn't be paying money up-front to agents, producers or casting directors. If your child gets cast in a film or TV show, the agent representing your child will take a standard 10% to 15% of the fee. The only expenses you should be paying after signing with an agent are photography fees to have your child's picture taken and printed.

If your child gets an audition, don't tell them how to read their lines. Casting directors are looking for true, natural instincts from kids. The best coaching you can do is to have your child work on the scenes, and to help with the listening exercise on page 17.

Some kids might want to explore the craft of acting just for fun, and that's a wonderful thing. Acting can help kids develop communication skills, creativity, confidence and self-awareness.

RESOURCES

For Young Actors

The Complete Film Dictionary, by Ira Konigsberg, Meridian Books

A Practical Handbook for the Actor, by Melissa Bruder, et al., Vintage Books

Acting Games, by Marsh Cassady, Meriwether Books

Comedy Improvisation, by Delton T. Horn, Meriwether Books

Child's Play, by Kerry Muir, Limelight Editions

The Young Actor's Workbook, by Judith Roberts Seto, Grove Press

For Acting Instructors and Parents

Word of Mouth: A Guide to Commercial Voice-Over Excellence, by Susan Blu and Molly Ann Mullin, Pomegranate Press Ltd.

Michael Caine: Acting in Film, by Michael Caine, Applause (book and video)

Teaching a Young Actor, by Renee Harmon, Walker & Co.

The Backstage Guide to Casting Directors, by Hette Lynne Hurtes, Backstage Books

Kids in the TV Commercial Biz, by Verree Watson Johnson, Wizards

Improve with Improv: A Guide to Improvisation and Character Development, by Brie Jones, Meriwether Books

Acting is Everything, by Judy Kerr, September Publishing

So You Want to Get Your Child into Commercials, by Susan Kramer and Kim Robert Walker, self-published
Mr. Kim Robert Walker
20945 Seacoast Circle
Huntington Beach, CA
92648 USA

Theatre Games for Young Performers, by Maria C. Novelly, Meriwether Books

Audition, by Michael Shurtleff, Bantam Books

Launching your Child in Showbiz: A Complete Step-by-Step Guide, by Dick Van Patten and Peter Berk, General Publishing Group Inc.

Services and Publications
In Canada

Canada on Location
Playback
KidScreen
all c/o Brunico Communications Inc.
366 Adelaide Street West, Suite 500
Toronto, Ontario M5V 1R9
phone (416) 408-2300

Directory of the Canadian Film, Television and Video Industry
Telefilm Canada Communications Dept.
Tour de la Banque Nationale
600 de la Gauchetiere St. W., 14th Floor
Montreal, Quebec H3B 4L8
phone (514) 283-6363

CFTPA Action Production Guide
Canadian Film & Television Production Association
175 Bloor St. E.
North Tower, Suite 806
Toronto, Ontario M4W 3R8
phone (416) 927-8942

Film Canada Yearbook
Cine-Communications
P.O. Box 152, Station R
Toronto, Ontario M4G 3Z3
phone (416) 696-2382

Who's Who in Canadian Film and Television
Academy of Canadian Cinema and Television
158 Pearl Street
Toronto, Ontario M5H 1L3
phone (416) 591-2040

In the United States

The Hollywood Reporter (daily)
5055 Wilshire Blvd
Los Angeles, CA 90036
phone (213) 525-2000

Daily Variety (daily)
5700 Wilshire Blvd
Los Angeles, CA 90036
phone (213) 857-6600

Backstage
P.O. Box 5017
Brentwood, Los Angeles, CA 90036

INDEX